How to...

BE A GENIUS

D1635575

How to...

BE A GENIUS

By JONATHAN HANCOCK

Illustrated by
Alan Rowe

OXFORD
UNIVERSITY PRESS

709760

For Phoebe, Alice and Maddie

OXFORD
UNIVERSITY PRESS

Great Clarendon Street, Oxford OX2 6DP

Oxford University Press is a department of the University of Oxford.
It furthers the University's objective of excellence in research, scholarship,
and education by publishing worldwide in

Oxford New York

Athens Auckland Bangkok Bogotá Buenos Aires Calcutta
Cape Town Chennai Dar es Salaam Delhi Florence Hong Kong Istanbul
Karachi Kuala Lumpur Madrid Melbourne Mexico City Mumbai
Nairobi Paris São Paulo Singapore Taipei Tokyo Toronto Warsaw
with associated companies in Berlin Ibadan

Oxford is a registered trade mark of Oxford University Press
in the UK and in certain other countries

Series devised by Hazel Richardson

Text copyright © Jonathan Hancock 2000
Illustrations copyright © Oxford University Press 2000
The moral rights of the author/artist have been asserted
First published 2000

British Library Cataloguing in Publication Data available

ISBN 0-19-910739-4

1 3 5 7 9 10 8 6 4 2

Printed in the United Kingdom

Contents

BECOMING A GENIUS

Anyone can make discoveries and come up with revolutionary inventions. It doesn't matter what school you go to, which subjects you're good at, how much money you've got or how old you are, as long as you start using your brain effectively you can achieve amazing things.

In this book you'll meet geniuses from many walks of life. You'll get to know scientists like Charles Darwin and Albert Einstein, who came up with incredible new ideas that changed the way people saw the world and the Universe for ever. You'll meet inventors like Thomas Edison, who thought up something new every ten days or so. And you'll look over the shoulder of the multi-talented artist, inventor and engineer Leonardo da Vinci, to see how he got things done.

All these geniuses were unique individuals, but if you look carefully you find out that they did have things in common. In this book you will get the chance to see how you measure up, and find out what to do to maximize your chances of becoming a great genius.

Follow the instructions to:

- test every area of your brain power

- predict how likely you are to become a famous genius

- find out how to have brilliant ideas

- learn about intelligence tests, and discover how to score top marks

- investigate the way computers think

- find out what makes someone a genius, and learn how you can become one too!

The secret ways that you can learn to think like a genius are revealed in this book – so get ready to boost *your* brainpower to brilliance!

WHAT IS A GENIUS?

$E = mc^2$. That's the bit most people know from Einstein's theories of relativity. It looks like a simple enough equation, but in fact the theories behind it are extremely complicated and they changed the way scientists saw time and space.

Einstein's discovery was phenomenal and breathtaking. Our understanding of the Universe changed for ever – and all thanks to a man who failed his school exams, never wore socks, and once even forgot where he lived!

Now is it 42, or 24?

Albert Einstein fits the image many people have of a genius. Not only did he achieve incredible things in physics, he also *looked* like a genius with his odd clothes and wild white hair. In one famous photograph he's sticking his tongue out at the camera, and there's a rascally glint in his eye.

He was an unusual character, and he had unusual thoughts – so unusual that he was able to make discoveries that no one had managed before. He was a genius because he achieved an entirely new level of thought. It's impossible to imagine anyone else coming up with $E = mc^2$.

But you don't have to be a scientist to be a genius. Here are a few more examples of genius at work.

See the Mona Lisa's smile, and you know immediately that Leonardo da Vinci painted with genius. No one else could have achieved that magic. Da Vinci took art to new levels, and even today his work opens our eyes to new discoveries about the world.

To lovers of classical music, Wolfgang Amadeus Mozart was unquestionably a genius. He did things with sound that no one else could do. His music continues to touch people's emotions in a way that's unique. Scientists have even discovered that listening to Mozart boosts your brainpower, so it seems that his genius is passed on through his work.

World Chess Champion Gary Kasparov uses his genius to take on the most powerful computers, often out-thinking them in ways that even the latest programs can't grasp.

Trevor Baylis invented a clockwork radio, and revolutionized the lives of millions of people in the developing world. His invention was itself a revolution, treating a common piece of equipment in an entirely new way. It seems a simple idea, but without the genius of this one special man perhaps no one would ever have invented it.

To be a genius, you need to be more than just good at what you do. You have to do it in a new and unique way. You must do more than teach or entertain or help other people. A true genius changes people's lives, and shows them that more is possible than they ever dreamed.

So it's not surprising that geniuses are often very odd people. Perhaps they *have* to be odd to come up with their unusually brilliant achievements. This book is about the strange men and women who have advanced our understanding of the world and our knowledge of what is possible.

You look odd enough to be a genius! Come in!

If you have a brain, you can be a genius – you just have to *learn to think like one*. The geniuses in this book emerged in different times, from a wide range of countries and backgrounds. They could have been ordinary, but they used their brains in extraordinary ways to become famous and to achieve great things. Follow these four simple but powerful rules and you too can become a genius.

The four keys to genius:

- start thinking creatively
- improve your memory
- boost your senses and co-ordination
- seize new opportunities for learning

You also need to develop some important *qualities* of genius, common to many of the great names featured in this book. You must have:

 unlimited interest in your chosen subjects and pursuits

 the persistence to succeed, despite any obstacles

 an ability to work with others

 the bravery to challenge even the experts, and to go further than anyone has gone before

The secrets of genius have fascinated us since ancient times. Various systems have been designed to measure thinking power and to identify potential geniuses. You're going to learn how to give your best performance in every kind of test.

CHAPTER TWO

TEST YOUR GENIUS

At the end of the book, the Genius Challenge will measure how close you are to being a genius. But first take a test to find out how strong your brain is now. Allow yourself no more than 20 minutes to do the test, then turn to page 19 to check the answers and find your current Genius Grade.

Become a genius— GENIUS TEST

WHAT YOU'LL NEED
* a pen
* paper
* a brain (preferably your own)

WHAT TO DO
Answer these questions and record your answers.

1 Observation
Can you spot the detail missing from each of these pictures?

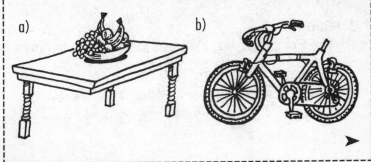

a) b)

➤

c)   d)

2 Words

a)   Which is the odd word out?

cup, saucer, plate, kitchen, bowl

b)   Which of the following words is the opposite of 'quiet'?

silent, very, noisy, still, fast

c)   Add one letter to make a familiar word:

T H I _ K I N G

d)   Which two words from the following list have the same meaning?

clever, honest, happy, trustworthy, beautiful

3 Numbers

a)   Which of the following numbers is different from the rest?

7, 3, 10, 5, 9

b)   Which of these number pairs is different from the rest?

6 3   8 1   2 7   4 8   9 0

➤

c) If 692 turns into 926, what does 715 turn into? Is it:

571, 517, 157 or 175?

d) What's the next number in the following sequence?

12 10 8 6 _

4 Shapes

a) Which shape comes next in the following sequence?

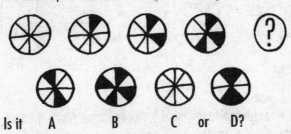

Is it   A   B   C   or   D?

b) If  turns into

what does 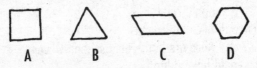 turn into?

Is it   A   B   C   or   D?

c) Which of the following shapes is the odd one out?

A   B   C   D

➤

d) Which one of the jigsaw pieces will fit the puzzle?

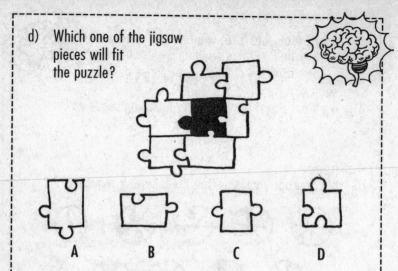

A   B   C   D

5 Memory

Read through the following 15 words for no more than one minute, then cover the page and see how many you can write down from memory, in any order:

hat, pen, clock, light, wall, book, blue, hole, short, mouse, heat, well, time, nail, line

6 Logic

Oliver is older than Daisy and Alice. Alice is older than Daisy. Oliver's brother is called Kim. Alice has an older sister. Daisy has no sisters.

From that information, which of the following statements are definitely true?

a) Daisy is younger than Alice
b) Oliver is older than Kim
c) Daisy is an only child
d) Daisy and Alice are friends
e) Daisy and Alice are both younger than Oliver
f) Alice could have a brother

➤

16

7 Creativity
What could the following diagram represent?
Write down as many different possibilities as you
can think of.

8 Senses
Give yourself an honest score, between 0 and 10 points, for
each of the following questions:
a) How varied is the music you listen to (from 0 for no music
   at all, to 10 for a completely varied musical collection)?
b) How much can you rely on your sense of smell?
c) How much enjoyment do you get from tasting different
   flavours?
d) How good is your eyesight?
e) How often do you do things that rely on delicate touch and
   a steady hand?
f) How much do you enjoy travelling to new places, with
   a variety of sights, sounds, tastes and smells?
g) How much interest do you have in birds, animals, plants,
   weather and the countryside?

9 Physical health
How often do you (answer either 'never', 'sometimes' or
'regularly' to each question):
a) raise your heartbeat for more than 20 minutes
   (e.g. swimming, running, cycling, fast walking)?
b) dance?
c) play precision sports like pool, archery, darts, golf or bowling?
d) practise flexibility and stretching?
e) work on your strength (e.g. lifting weights, doing press-ups,
   throwing the javelin)?

➤

f) practise your balance (e.g. gymnastics, tai chi, circus skills)?

g) work on your hand-eye co-ordination (e.g. juggling, computer games)?

10 Interests

a) Think of being at school. Write down all the lessons that you find interesting.

b) Now write down all things you do outside school that you find interesting.

c) And now write down anything else that you would like to do or find out about, but that you haven't got round to yet.

11 Teamwork

How many different people (e.g. teacher, parent, sister, friend, uncle, neighbour) would you ask for help with:

a) your homework?

b) your hobbies?

c) ideas you have?

12 Persistence

Answer the following questions with either 'no' or 'yes':

a) Do you have any hobbies that you've enjoyed for more than a year?

b) Have any of your friendships lasted for more than three years?

c) If you have difficulties with your schoolwork, do you keep trying until you find a solution?

d) Have you ever taken part in a sponsored event, and completed the challenge?

e) Do you regularly get to the end of books?

Find your genius grade

0–100 points: Genius Grade 1 – very weak

101–150 points: Genius Grade 2 – poor

151–200 points: Genius Grade 3 – average

201–250 points: Genius Grade 4 – good

251–300 points: Genius Grade 5 – very good

301–350 points or more: Genius Grade 6 – excellent

351 points or more: Genius Grade 7 – outstanding:
true genius material

CHAPTER THREE

BEGINNINGS OF GENIUS

Anyone can become a genius, but for some the journey to greatness is more of a struggle than for others. It certainly helps if you have a supportive family, help from a company or organization, an inspiring place to live and a supportive community. But these are by no means essential. As you'll see, a difficult upbringing sometimes helps! It can be just what someone needs to make them determined to succeed against all the odds. As for the lucky ones –

Genius in the genes?............................

Do you have any high-IQ jeans?

No, not those sort of jeans!

Some geniuses seem to have been born to greatness as members of very clever and illustrious families. This doesn't guarantee future success, but it provides a very helpful starting-point.

Genius families

Part I: Sicily, 3rd century BC

Archimedes was born into one of the most famous families in Sicily in 287 BC. Some people say he was related to the ruler, Hiero. Archimedes' father, Pheidias, was an astronomer who was already thinking big thoughts, trying to get to grips with the dimensions of the Universe. This seems to have sparked Archimedes' imagination, and he set out on a long career of exploration, trying to answer some big questions of his own about maths and sciences. He made many important discoveries, paving the way for all the physicists and mechanics who came after him.

That's Dad, measuring the Universe again!

Genius families
Part II: Germany, 18th century AD

Johann Sebastian Bach was born into a musical family, but he still had to struggle for his success. His elder brother Johann Christian was a skilful organist, and taught him to play at an early age. But for some reason J.C. refused to share his collection of books. So the young J.S. used to sneak in during the hours of darkness and copy the books he needed by the light of the Moon! Even though he was a renowned singer, violinist, organist and composer by the age of 19, J.S. still did everything he could to improve. It's said that he once travelled to see a famous organist perform more than 250 miles away, and made the entire round trip on foot.

Bach became one of the greatest classical composers of all time. He had a helpful family background, but he was also one of the hardest-working composers in history. At the height of his career he was playing for church services, looking after a school, writing music to order, and composing and rehearsing a complicated piece of music for his choir every single week.

Let's see – choir rehearsal, church service, write organ voluntary, school staff meeting – a quiet day today.

Genius organizations............................

Many great thinkers and creators found it helpful to join groups of like-minded people. Often they worked hard to get into the most supportive and inspiring organizations and societies.

Choose your friends
Part I: Egypt, 3rd century BC

Archimedes moved from Sicily to Egypt to study at the mathematical school in Alexandria. There he built up friendships with many local scientists. He also enjoyed setting puzzles for his fellow students and taking part in thinking games.

What do you think of this? I got it off my friend Rubik.

The great Italian painter and inventor Leonardo da Vinci was lucky enough to be taught by a master artist called Verrocchio. Verrocchio was able to put him in touch with many of the most talented local people, and later he joined the Company of Saint Luke, a guild of scientists and artists.

Choose your friends
Part II: Oxford, England, around 1650 AD

Christopher Wren is one of the most famous architects in history. He designed St Paul's Cathedral in London, as well as hundreds of other amazing structures.

He was also a great scientist and astronomer, and spent his life working his way into the country's most prestigious organizations.

After leaving school at 14 and working in several jobs, Wren made it to Oxford University in his mid-teens. At Oxford he met many supremely clever thinkers, and some of them later helped him to found the Royal Society, an organization designed to encourage great discoveries. His colleagues there included Isaac Newton, the genius who made important discoveries about light, maths, and, most famously, gravity.

Genius places ....

Some cities and countries have proved to be great places for encouraging geniuses. Archimedes, for example, studied in the great library in Alexandria, and Leonardo da Vinci gained greatly from his time in the inspiring cities of Florence and Milan. Florence was a particularly good place for any would-be genius to hang out. It was at the centre of a number of regions and welcomed travellers from far afield. It maintained a healthy rivalry with nearby cities like Venice and Rome. And there were plenty of other clever, ambitious people there for Leonardo to learn from.

Albert Einstein had two favourite places to work: Oxford in England and Princeton in the USA. He said he liked the architecture and the light, and found both places to be quiet, friendly university towns where he could work happily and productively.

Genius times

Some periods in history have been particularly good for aspiring geniuses. If your particular genius leads you to build a time-machine one day, you might like to set the controls for some of these inspiring destinations.

The right place, the right time
Part 1: Greece, 5th century BC

This was a prosperous age, and one very rich in geniuses. Visit here and you'll meet Aeschylus, Sophocles and Euripides, great playwrights at a time when poetry and drama were treated as sporting events! They all had amazing records of success in the fiercely-fought competitions.

And in the red corner...

They were all famous philosophers too. They used their understanding of human behaviour to write plays that are thrilling, bloody and often terrifying. Their plays are still performed today. You'll also meet Socrates, the philosopher who asked the biggest question of them all: how do we really know what's true and what isn't? He made people question all their old beliefs, and changed the world by inventing logical thinking.

The right place, the right time

Part II: Italy, 15th century AD

Another wealthy place. Hundreds of thousands of people had been killed off by the Black Death, the terrible plague that swept through Europe in the 14th century. Afterwards all the riches were shared among far fewer people, so there were more opportunities for geniuses to advance themselves. This was a time when art, philosophy and invention all flourished. We call it the Renaissance, or 'rebirth'.

One of the key figures of the Renaissance in Italy was Michelangelo. He became the most famous sculptor in history, and was also a genius painter and architect. He spent four years painting the ceiling of the Sistine Chapel in Rome, one of the most ambitious and impressive artworks ever completed.

Other Italian geniuses of the Renaissance were the painters Raphael and Titian, the political writer and thinker Machiavelli, and one of the greatest geniuses of all time, Leonardo da Vinci, who was also an inventor, engineer, botanist, weather-forecaster, musician... There was excitement in the air, the buzz of new discoveries, ideas and possibilities. And there were plenty of rich people around to buy their paintings. Leonardo was born at the right time in a place perfectly suited to encouraging his awesome genius.

The right place, the right time
Part III: England, 16th century AD

The geniuses from this period owe a great debt of thanks to their ruler, the much-loved Queen Elizabeth I. She believed she had to be an inspiration to the nation, and made sure that pictures of her were distributed far and wide. She gathered at court the greatest minds, chose her advisors carefully, and led England through many perilous years. Her brilliance as a ruler allowed other geniuses to flourish, like the philosopher Francis Bacon, and the most famous writer of all time, William Shakespeare. He made the most of the age he was born into, with its explosion of knowledge, foreign influences and new ideas. He wrote the best-loved plays in history, and changed theatre for ever.

How likely are you to follow in the footsteps of Socrates, Michelangelo and Shakespeare? Complete the following questionnaire to check your pedigree as an aspiring genius.

Become a genius—
CHECK YOUR BACKGROUND

WHAT YOU'LL NEED
* a pen
* paper

WHAT TO DO
Answer the following questions.

1 Families
Do you have...

a relative who went to college or university, to give you advice on your future career?

a family tradition of a particular kind of work, or a family business, to get you started?

grandparents to talk to, for their wisdom and experience?

family holidays or days out, so that you can learn from new people and places?

2 Organizations
Are you a member of...

a school or college, to get help from teachers and schoolfriends?

any after-school classes, for extra inspiration?

a library, to help you build up your knowledge?

a club or society, for specific learning and training?

3 Places
Do you have...

a college or university in your nearest town, to create an atmosphere of learning?

➤

a museum within five kilometres, for information?

an art gallery within ten kilometres, for inspiration?

countryside or a park nearby, for quiet thought?

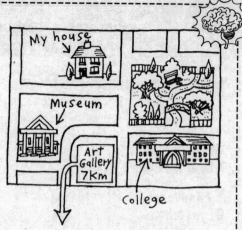

4 Times

In this day and age, do you think that...

anyone can be successful, as long as they try hard enough?

everyone can try foreign foods, and books, music and films from around the world?

we can all find ways of accessing the Internet, at home, in school, or by visiting a library?

telephones, faxes and emails are easy to use and available everywhere?

Check your success

Give yourself one point every time you answer 'yes' to a question.

0–4 points:  It's going to be a struggle for you to become a genius, but it is still possible. Bach was committed enough to overcome his difficulties, Leonardo was born to a peasant girl in a small town, but still rose to greatness – and so can you.

5–8 points: You have an average chance of achieving the rank of genius. There are probably more opportunities for boosting your brainpower than you think, so keep your eyes open every day.

9–12 points: You stand a better chance than most of making it to the top. Don't be afraid to go that little bit further in your quest for genius. You need to stay focused on your goals.

13–16 points: You have the perfect background for becoming a genius – and you have to make the most of it. Many other hopefuls have shown early promise, then fallen by the wayside. Keep up your enthusiasm and determination, and make use of everything and everyone you've got!

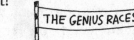

CHAPTER FOUR

DISCOVERIES AND INVENTIONS

It only takes a moment of genius to change the world, as long as you're brave enough to take a few risks.

Four rules of invention, plus another four, makes... seven?

You too can change the world with your genius. Just study the Eight Secrets of Invention and you will be well on your way

1 Delight in your chosen subjects ....

Most of the geniuses in this book were completely gripped by their subject. Some longed to find the answers to questions, or solve problems, that had puzzled people for years, sometimes centuries. Others pursued new ideas or creative visions that only they could see.

The patient clockmaker
England, 18th century

John Harrison solved the 'longitude problem', one of the great puzzles of the 18th century. He invented a clock that could measure time at sea (where pendulum clocks are useless), and which made it possible for sailors to calculate their position east or west (their longitude) accurately for the first time. It was a problem that had baffled many great thinkers, and he pursued a solution with incredible determination. This was only possible because of his love of invention and experimentation.

When he was still a teenager, he demonstrated this love of learning when a visiting clergyman loaned him a textbook he'd been eager to read. Instead of just leafing through it, he wrote it out, word for word. He copied and labelled every diagram and even added his own extra notes.

But if you'd asked me, I have a spare copy...

Still doing your homework?

England, 1963

When a 10-year-old called Andrew Wiles was walking home one day, he called into his local library. There he read a book that would change his life, because in it was one of the greatest mathematical puzzles of all time, called 'Fermat's Last Theorem'. The mathematician Pierre Fermat once wrote that he had discovered the answer to a tricky problem, but he never wrote it down — and nobody since had been able to offer a solution. Andrew Wiles was so intrigued by the idea that he decided to crack the puzzle himself. He loved maths riddles, and his delight in the subject gave him all the energy he needed to get going on his quest.

Thirty-four years later, on 27 June 1997, he collected a prize of $50,000 for solving a conundrum that had baffled the world for more than 350 years. His interest in it had kept him going, and his delight in maths only grew stronger with each setback.

2 Learn from those who've gone before

Geniuses think new thoughts and dream up original ideas, but they need to start with the information already available. They must be able to learn from their predecessors.

In ancient Greece, each great thinker learned from the last. Socrates taught Plato, the 'grandfather of philosophy', who taught Aristotle, the inventor of logical reasoning, who in turn taught Alexander the Great, perhaps the most powerful ruler in history.

In his early 20s, Albert Einstein sent out letter after letter asking famous scientists to take him on as an assistant so that he could learn from them. Not one of them replied. Instead he had to read as many of their books as he could get hold of.

When Einstein's career later took off, he made use of the discoveries of two particular geniuses from the past, Isaac Newton and James Clerk Maxwell. These men had very different theories about time and space, but Einstein took a fresh look at them and came up with a new way of looking at the Universe: his General Theory of Relativity, including $E = mc^2$.

Pay great attention to the work others have done before you, because only then will you be able to take it a step further.

3 Learn your subject matter thoroughly

Once you've decided on the areas that interest you, do everything you can to learn all there is to know about them. But don't restrict yourself: read and learn as widely as possible. Here are just some of the varied subjects that great geniuses have studied.

William Shakespeare:
history, languages, law,
literature, maths, music,
politics, psychology,
science, sport.

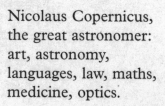

Nicolaus Copernicus,
the great astronomer:
art, astronomy,
languages, law, maths,
medicine, optics.

Leonardo da Vinci: acoustics, anatomy, aquanautics, botany, conjuring, geology, horses, geometry, mechanics, music, painting, sculpture, weather-forecasting.

Martha Graham, the American ballet dancer and choreographer, whose brilliance changed dance for ever: animals, art, history, literature, myths and legends, poetry, psychology, religion.

Geniuses are good at finding inspiration in everything they read and learn about. They are naturally inquisitive, and build up huge stores of information on many different subjects. To be a genius in any one subject you need to harvest information from many fields. Read widely, then focus your knowledge in the direction of your genius.

4 The power of co-operation ....

There are many famous genius partnerships and groups. Great thinkers seem to be naturally drawn to other great thinkers, and together they can achieve amazing things.

Francis Crick and James Watson worked together to unravel the structure of DNA, the complicated chemical that contains the biological 'blueprint' for every living being. Watson got Crick interested in

DNA, they bounced ideas off each other, argued over many different theories, and eventually made their joint discovery through powerful teamwork. Together they revolutionized biology, and our understanding of human life.

Since we're Crick and Watson, can't we call it C'n'W?

Orville and Wilbur Wright worked together to build the first aeroplanes. Marie Curie formed a team with her husband Pierre, and they made crucial discoveries about radioactivity and X-rays. Even Michelangelo had a team behind him when he painted the Sistine Chapel. He's the only name people remember, but there were in fact many other people working with him.

Find friends who are interested in the same things as you, and work with them to give even more energy to your work.

5 Create a thinking zone ....

Put some thought into where you do your best thinking. Geniuses often use particular 'thinking zones' to boost their brainpower.

The great French novelist Marcel Proust lined his workroom with cork to create perfect silence. British dictionary writer Samuel Johnson did his best work listening to the purring of his cat!

Perhaps you prefer listening to music while you work. If so, try Mozart. Recent research suggests that listening to Mozart's music can boost intelligence and creativity.

Some geniuses find that water helps them think. Einstein was a keen sailor, and the modern-day inventor Trevor Baylis has many of his best ideas while he's in the swimming-pool. A Japanese inventor called Naka Mats holds his breath and sinks under-water when he needs to do some really deep thinking.

So why don't I have any good ideas?

Mats also has a whole range of different coloured rooms for tackling different kinds of problems. It must work, because his inventions have made him a billionaire!

Where you think can be an important factor in how well you think.

6 Ask the right questions ....

Questioning is a very important part of inventing. Here are some of the most useful things you can ask:

 What can be added? A chemist once knocked over a bottle of collodion, a plastic substance. The collodion stuck some of the bits of broken bottle together. He realized that it could be added to glass to make it safer. Now many panes of glass have a plastic layer in the middle, thanks to the chemist's clever idea.

 How else could this be used? In 1971 Bob Brown was tinkering with an electric guitar in his garage. He accidentally crossed two wires and there was a high-pitched shriek of sound – which sent a group of rats scurrying away in terror. Bob realized that his amplifying equipment could be put to another use, and he designed a gadget for repelling rats. He's now a millionaire.

What can be adapted? A waffle-seller at the 1905 World's Fair spotted an ice-cream stand nearby, and had a brilliant idea. He moulded one of his flat waffles into a cone, filled it with ice cream – and the rest is history.

 What if nothing is done? When Clarence Crane's mint-making machine went wrong and started stamping holes in the mints, he could have thrown them all away and started again. But instead he spotted that these new mints-with-holes were even better, and now around 30 billion packets are sold every year.

 Can the same thing be done more cheaply? Antoine Feuchtwanger was selling sausages in America in the 1880s. Rather than give customers at his stand plates and cutlery, he wanted to save money – and washing-up – so Antoine started selling the sausages inside bread rolls. And so the hot dog was born!

Geniuses are constantly asking questions. Can it be done faster, made bigger, combined with other ideas, rearranged?

Don't worry about the right answers: first make sure you're asking the right questions.

7 Be ready for revelation......................

When something catches your interest, it may be telling you something important.

Galileo, the Italian mathematician, physicist and astronomer, was day-dreaming in church when he spotted a chandelier swaying from side to side. Suddenly something clicked in his brain, and he knew the answer to the laws ruling how pendulums swing.

It's also vital that you recognize your winning ideas. Great thoughts can occur any time, any place.

Archimedes was supposedly in the bath when he had one of his best ideas, inspired by the way the water-level moved up the bath as he got in. He shouted 'Eureka!' ('I've found it!'), and was so excited that he forgot he wasn't wearing any clothes, and ran down the road stark naked!

8 Publicize your discoveries ....

In 1482 Leonardo da Vinci wrote a long letter to a nobleman in Milan, asking for a job. In the letter he described some of his inventions and ideas, including:

* portable bridges
* ladders
* cannons
* tanks
* catapults
* viaducts
* sculptures

Not surprisingly, he got the job.

43

After Trevor Baylis created the first clockwork radio, he spent years letting people know about his invention. When he eventually found people interested in backing him, there was another round of publicity and promotion to find people to make it. He took part in radio and television programmes to help raise interest, until eventually his idea was recognized for the work of genius that it was. He now has his own successful factories around the world, and his radios relay information and entertainment to millions of people in the developing world.

Once you're sure of your inventions and ideas, tell people about them.

CHAPTER FIVE

TESTING FOR GENIUS

How do you measure genius? The great men and women who appear in this book all accomplished incredible things, and proved their genius in many different ways. So is it ever possible to measure intelligence, if it comes in so many different forms?

First of all you have to decide what intelligence is. And that depends on where you live!

If you grew up in some areas of Africa or the Pacific Islands, you might well be taught that intelligence is how good you are at talking to other people and getting on with them. In these traditional cultures, fast thinking is not always best. In fact, in the Baganda tribe in Uganda, the cleverest people are thought to be those who act slowly and cautiously, making very careful decisions. The Bagandan word for intelligence is *ngware*, which means being slow, careful and straightforward.

... and I'm looking for the last person to press their buzzer ...

On the other hand, the Western world tends to value speed of thought. We have developed tests that measure people's skill at giving answers to written questions, within a time limit.

Perhaps you've heard of IQ tests?

I Q and Q and Q...

IQ stands for 'intelligence quotient', and these tests were developed to try to measure people's brainpower. They were designed to be used by teachers to assess their students, by employers keen to find clever people to work for them, and by anyone who wants to find out how intelligent they are.

The first tests were created in the early 1900s by a Frenchmen called Alfred Binet. He had noticed that most of the people making it to university were from the upper classes, and he thought that this was unfair.

He saw the need for a system to measure cleverness that had nothing to do with how much factual information someone had been able to learn, or the educational opportunities they had had. Binet invented what he hoped would be a fair test of a person's brainpower.

Binet decided to see how good people were at basic word, number and shape puzzles, and to find out how comfortable they were with language. His tests also took age into account.

IQ tests work out your mental age, which may well be different from your real age. For example, a clever 10-year-old could have a mental age of 12. Measuring people against others of the same age produces IQ scores. The average IQ is 100, and the higher your score, the cleverer you are supposed to be.

Unfortunately, these tests can only measure certain skills, and some people think that they're not very accurate. If you're shown the tricks, you can boost your score – so perhaps people with high IQs are just good at doing IQ tests! Alfred Binet hoped his tests would be used to chart children's progress in school, but many people today are concerned that the tests label some children as not being very clever, rather than helping them to improve. Binet would not have liked that. He knew that his tests only measured a certain sort of intelligence.

IQ tests are still used today, and it's useful to be good at them – but IQ isn't everything. It's important to remember that many of the geniuses in this book probably wouldn't have done very well with them! Einstein, for example, was bad at maths, so he may have had difficulty solving some of the puzzles.

If you have to take an IQ test, here are some tips to help you do your best. In fact, you can try these tips whatever sort of mental challenge you're tackling.

Tip 1   Think positively

Tackle each question enthusiastically, try to enjoy the test, and don't let nerves hold you back. Treat the test as a fun challenge.

Tip 2   Relax your mind

Before you start, spend a few moments with your eyes closed, breathing deeply and slowly to calm your mind. It might help to picture yourself in a nice, relaxing place. Try to imagine all the colours you can see, the sounds you can hear, and let your imagination come alive. It's important to go into any test with your mind open and working creatively. But don't get TOO relaxed!

Tip 3   Check the clock

Most IQ tests have to be completed in a certain amount of time, so you need to know how long you've got. Always make sure you know how quickly you need to work. Don't go so fast that you make silly mistakes, but don't waste time.

Tip 4   Read the questions carefully

Many people lose marks simply by misreading a question. Don't assume that you know what a question means straight away. Read it through a couple of times to be absolutely sure.

Tip 5   Doodle

Many great geniuses, like the painter Picasso, the explorer Christopher Columbus and the composer Beethoven, used to jot down their thoughts in doodles and scribbles. Always make sure that you have some rough paper for making notes and trying out different answers. You might use coloured pens to help you think creatively.

Tip 6 Work out what sort of question it is

Most IQ tests use the same basic questions, and you can become familiar with the main types. Here are four of the most popular types of question:

a) Odd one out

In these questions, you are given a group of words, numbers or shapes, and asked to spot the one that doesn't fit. This means that all but one of the items have something in common. You need to work what that thing is, so that you can spot the one item that's different.

For example:
Which is the odd one out?

> lion, spaniel, tiger, cheetah, leopard

The answer is: spaniel. Four of the animals have something in common: lion, tiger, cheetah and leopard are all types of big cat. A spaniel, on the other hand, is a type of dog – so the spaniel must be the odd one out.

Sometimes the answer is easy to spot, but often you have to think very carefully, and run through lots of possibilities in your head. Just keep asking yourself questions until inspiration hits.

For example:
Which is the odd one out?

hair, pipe, hill, bucket, comb

You might ask yourself:
'Is this something to do with heads?', because 'hair' and 'comb' are on the list – but none of the other words seems to fit.

'Is there a connection with water?', because both the bucket and the pipe might carry water – but again none of the other words ties in.

'Perhaps it's got something to do with the way the words are written?' IQ questions can be a bit tricky, so it's always worth looking for something a little devious. In this case, you'll spot that all of the words except one have the same number of letters, giving you the odd one out: 'bucket'.

b) Same/opposite

Here you have to show that you know when words mean the same thing, and when words have opposite meanings. Always read these questions especially carefully.

For example:
Which of the following words is the opposite of 'strong'?
muscle, head, weak, empty, sad

Often there are words in the list to confuse you, like 'muscle'. Your mind will tell you instantly that there is a connection between 'strong' and 'muscle', but is it the right connection? You're looking for the opposite of 'strong', so muscle isn't the answer. It often helps to put the word in a sentence, or several different sentences. If a strong man lost his power, he would be ...? If the coffee wasn't very strong, you might call it ...? If I wasn't strong at football, I would be ...? Asking all these questions would point straight to the answer: 'weak'.

Another example:
Which of the following words means the same as 'saw'?
scissors, watched, blue, kite, angry

Scissors are a bit like a saw, because they both cut things – but not exactly the same, so that can't be the answer. In fact, none of the words seems to be like a saw, so perhaps this is a different kind of 'saw'?

Try putting it in some other sentences:
'I saw my friend.' 'You saw him
on television.'
As soon as you do this,
you'd realize that the
word 'watched' will also
fit in the same sentences:
'I watched my friend.'
'You watched him on
television.' So 'watched'
must be the right answer.

c) This becomes that
If 2 becomes 4, then 6 becomes – what?
10, 12, 13 or 16

The answer is 12. To solve this sort of question, you must work out how one thing becomes another. What has happened to 2 for it to become 4? Has it had 2 added to it? If so, you would have to add 2 to 6 to get the answer – but 8 isn't there in the list of possible solutions, so that can't be it.

If you double 2 it becomes 4, so perhaps you have to double 6 to find the answer. Is 12 there in the list? Yes! So 12 must be the right answer.

Sometimes these questions are written like this:
'but' is to 'tub' as 'pan' is to – what?
hat, nip, top or nap

'Is to' is just the same as 'becomes'. Just ask yourself: if the word 'but' turns into the word 'tub', what happens to it? The answer is that it is written backwards, so you have to do the same thing to 'pan' to come up with the solution: 'nap'.

d) Patterns and sequences
In these questions you are given a sequence of numbers, letters, words or shapes, and you have to decide what comes next. To solve them, you need to work out what sort of sequence it is.

For example:
What comes next in the following sequence?

a e i m q

Is it b u z n *or* r?

If you count how many letters there are between a and e in the alphabet, you'll find that it's three. There are also three letters between e and i, i and m, and so on. So there must be three letters between q and the next letter in the sequence. The answer has to be: u.

Here's another example:
Which shape comes next?

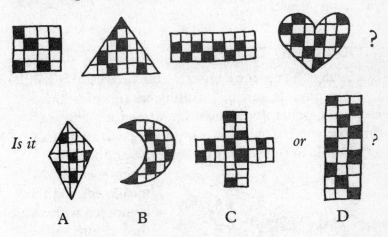

How does the sequence work? If you look carefully you'll see that each shape has one more section filled in than the last. It's as simple as that. It has nothing to do with the shapes themselves. (I told you IQ tests could be devious!) When you know what's happening, you can easily work out that the next shape must have nine spaces filled in, so the answer must be:

Whatever type of question you're tackling, try approaching it from different angles until you can crack it.

Ask yourself questions, explore your hunches, try different possibilities. Be persistent, keep an open mind, and you might surprise yourself how often you shout 'Eureka!'.

Well, you said approach problems from different angles!

Another way to test.............................

Research is being done into the link between IQ and reaction time. In one test, volunteers sit in front of an electronic panel. Bulbs light up at random, and each time the volunteers must move their hand as quickly as possible to push a button underneath the bulb.

Their speed is measured, and then compared with their results on written IQ tests.

From experiments like this it seems that people with fast reactions are also quick at solving written puzzles. Try it yourself.

56

Become a genius—
REACT FAST!

WHAT YOU'LL NEED
* a ruler, preferably 30 cm long
* a friend

WHAT TO DO
1   Hold one arm straight out in front of you.
2   Ask your friend to hold the ruler by one end while the
    1 cm mark hangs between — but not touching — your
    open thumb and first finger.
3   Your friend lets go of the ruler.
4   You have to catch it between your fingers as quickly as
    possible, before it falls right through and hits the floor.
5   When you catch the ruler, look to see where your fingers
    are. How many centimetres have gone through? Try it
    three times, and record your best result, then let the rest
    of your friends have a go. Who has the fastest reaction
    time? Perhaps one of you is a genius in the making!

CHAPTER SIX

BRAIN VERSUS COMPUTER

Can computers become geniuses? That's a question that many top brains are working on right now. Ever since the 1950s, the idea of AI or artificial intelligence has fascinated scientists. They have built computers that can do more and more complicated operations – but have they taught them to think?

One of the inventors of the computer, the genius mathematician Alan Turing, came up with a way to test a computer's thinking ability:

The Turing Test

The rules of the Turing test are as follows:

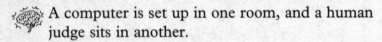 A computer is set up in one room, and a human judge sits in another.

The judge 'talks' to the computer by typing questions and answers on a keyboard.

Sometimes another human takes control of the computer in the sealed room and has a conversation with the judge. At other times the computer itself communicates.

The judge is never told whether he is talking to the computer or to another human.

So can he tell the difference?

To beat the Turing Test, a computer has to fool the judge into thinking that he is talking to an intelligent human being.

But isn't there more to it?

Sophisticated programs now allow computers to do extremely well in the Turing Test. For short periods they can seem just like humans. There are still some things that confuse them, though, because conversations are much more complicated than you might imagine.

Think of two friends telling a joke, for example. How would you teach a computer that 'Why did the chicken cross the road?' is funny?

This is one of the reasons why some scientists say computers will never manage to become intelligent.

Our thinking relies a great deal on feelings and emotions. Computers don't have emotions. For example, you could store your favourite book in a computer's memory, then make the computer search it for a particular word. It would look like the computer was reading, but it would be very different from you reading the book. The computer wouldn't feel excited or scared or amused. It wouldn't know if the story was good or bad. It wouldn't have feelings about the information, so it would only look like it was intelligent.

Computers can do impressive things, but intelligent humans have to give them the instructions first. After all, when you listen to the radio you don't think that the radio set is intelligent, even though it seems to be performing amazing pieces of music!

The phenomenal thing is that computers today are unbelievably fast and powerful, yet the human brain is still the winner in most tests of thinking power.

Computers can churn through millions of operations every second, hour after hour, without getting tired or making a mistake. Our brains can't compete with that level of performance, but often we don't need to. We can decide where to focus our thoughts. We can find shortcuts, use our feelings, and go with our hunches. The human brain can also process many different kinds of information: sounds, colours, smells, textures, and do a number of things at once.

In many challenging situations, only the amazing brain has got what it takes to succeed. Genius thinking is much more than sheer processing power.

Checkmate ....

The Deep Blue computer program could look at 500 million chess moves every second. It was programmed with all the famous chess games, and all the latest ideas. In 1996 a match was held between Deep Blue and the World Chess Champion Garry Kasparov.

It seems unbelievable, but Kasparov was favourite to win – and he did. He led the computer into complicated situations in which its memory power and speed simply weren't enough. Only the human player could get a sense of the right moves and put together a winning plan.

In 1998, there was a rematch. Deep Blue – now called Deeper Blue – had been made even more powerful. It could look at 1000 million moves every second. This time the computer won. Kasparov put up a brave fight, but eventually lost by 3 points to 2. So he still came close, even with all that brute electronic force up against him.

The next world champion may well be a computer program, but computers will surely push humans' ability in chess to new levels. And it will still be a long time before a computer can write a book about chess, or decide of its own accord to play – or enjoy making the winning move!

How computers can boost your brainpower ....

You can use your computer, or those in your school or local library, to boost your own chances of becoming a genius.

Great thinkers have always been willing to use the latest technology. Beethoven, for example, made use of the newly invented metronome to make sure his pieces were performed at exactly the right tempos. Never be afraid of new gadgets. They don't replace human brainpower, but they can let you keep your energy for the most important bits of thinking.

For example, if you were planning a new look for your bedroom, you could use a calculator to check the measurements and calculations. This would save your brainpower for dreaming up new design ideas.

If you play chess, draughts, backgammon or bridge, use computers to give you the ultimate challenge. It's a great way to learn and improve, because you can keep increasing the skill level and pushing yourself to play better. When the computer wins, try to see how it does it. Learn from your own mistakes. Trust your judgement, and keep challenging even the most powerful machines.

Use the Internet to build up your knowledge and to explore the areas that interest you. Geniuses communicate with other experts, so you can send emails and chat online to swap ideas and gain inspiration from others.

You can even spend some of your time playing computer games to improve your reflexes and problem-solving ability. You could try the reaction-time experiment on page 57, before and after playing a computer game for 15 minutes, to see whether your reflexes have improved!

CHAPTER SEVEN

GENIUS CHARACTERS

Even the most powerful computer in the world can't be a genius, because it has no character. It can remember and calculate quickly and accurately, and handle huge amounts of information – but it can't think about the information like we can. It has no feelings, no opinions, no moments of madness.

Investigate the great human geniuses and you'll see that they all have special parts to their character, qualities which allow them to go beyond everything previously achieved. Their lives hold many of the secrets of having great ideas and putting them into practice. Learn from their examples to boost your own chances of becoming a genius. To be a genius you need to –

– have fun ....

Leonardo da Vinci was well known for his jokes and funny stories. Galileo had a busy social life and was another great joker. Bill Gates, the world's richest man and the genius behind the huge Microsoft company, has been described as 'a perpetual teenager'. He once said that one of his favourite hobbies was playing with earth-moving equipment on building sites!

– be inquisitive ....

Geniuses spend their lives asking questions about the world around them.

Leonardo da Vinci filled many notebooks with his explorations. Here's a snippet:

> 'I roamed the countryside searching for answers to things I did not understand. Why shells existed on the tops of mountains ... why the thunder lasts a longer time than that which causes it ... how the various circles of water form around the spot which has been struck by a stone ... why a bird sustains itself in the air ...'

The typical genius questions are why and how.

– be brave...

Geniuses simply can't be afraid of making mistakes.
Orville and Wilbur Wright had many crashes and
ruined many aeroplanes before they finally got off the
ground. Inventor Thomas Edison failed literally
thousands of times before he managed to turn
electricity into light. He told his friends that, because
he knew so many ways that didn't work, he was
much closer than any other inventor to finding the
right answer!

Geniuses must also be prepared to cause shocks. New
ideas can seem strange and even frightening to others,
and great thinkers are often described as disruptive
and rebellious.

– keep trying ....

Thomas Edison once said
that genius was 'one per
cent inspiration and
ninety-nine per cent
perspiration'.

To become a
genius you
must be
prepared
to work
long and
hard, often
in the face
of great
obstacles.

– be inspired ....

The answers you're looking for may be close by – you just have to know where to look.

Leonardo da Vinci wandered through the countryside looking at nature, and many other great thinkers have found their inspiration there too. Travel is another good source of inspiration. Mozart picked up many good musical ideas during his travels. While still in his teens, Albert Einstein persuaded his parents to let him tour the main cities of Italy. He came back with some exciting ideas.

Tips for helping you be inspired

- Spend time in nature, looking at the way animals and plants behave.

- Take every opportunity you get to travel, both in this country and abroad.

- Start a scrapbook: fill it with photographs, leaves, newspaper cuttings, tickets – everything that reminds you of your most interesting experiences.

– stay fit...

There's an ancient saying, *mens sana in corpore sano*, which means 'a healthy mind in a healthy body'. It's very important for you to feel good and for your body to be operating at its best, so that your mind can also function powerfully.

As well as being a genius philosopher, poet and statesman, Sophocles was also a champion athlete and won many trophies.

Inventor Trevor Baylis swims every morning, and was a champion in his youth. Top mathematician Ronald Graham is an expert trampolinist, bowler and tennis player. Leonardo da Vinci was famous for his strength, agility, and special ability as a horseman. World Chess Champion Garry Kasparov spends as much time training his body – running, swimming and lifting weights – as his incredible brain.

Genius keep-fit.....................................

Aerobic exercise: Your brain makes up only 3 per cent of your bodyweight, but it uses an amazing 30 per cent of the oxygen you breathe in. It's vital that your brain is supplied with plenty of oxygen. Swimming, fast walking, running, football, tennis and other sports like these improve what's called your aerobic fitness – your ability to take in oxygen. Exercise can double your aerobic fitness.

Strength: Kasparov has said that the stronger he feels, the stronger he thinks. Boosting your physical strength makes you feel more positive and improves your persistence and stamina. Under careful supervision you can use weights, or practise field sports like the javelin and discus, to improve your strength. Leonardo da Vinci was said to be able to bend horseshoes with his bare hands!

Flexibility: Leonardo was also described as graceful and poised. He had studied the way the human body works, and made sure that his worked without strain. If you've ever pulled a muscle or strained some part of your body, you'll know how much mental energy this takes away. To have free, creative thoughts it's important to feel free, supple and relaxed.

Before sitting down to work or think, spend a few minutes loosening up. Slowly roll your head, clockwise and anticlockwise. Shake your arms and legs. Carefully bend down to touch your toes, then stretch your arms up towards the ceiling. Do this a few times before you get started – and again every so often while you're hard at work.

Balance: Gymnastics, rollerblading and skate-boarding are all excellent ways of improving your balance. Check your balance now simply by standing on one leg. How long can you stand like that without falling over? Leonardo was described by people who knew him as balanced and graceful. His body was under his control just as completely as his mind.

Diet: Your diet must also be properly balanced. Make sure you supply your brain with all the nutrients it needs to work well. Eat a diet low in fats and sugar, rich in fresh fruit and vegetables, and drink plenty of water. Never eat so much that you feel full and tired, but be sure to keep up your energy levels right through the day. Savour the food that you eat – how it looks and smells as well as tastes – and make every mealtime an inspiring, relaxing, refuelling event.

Become a genius—
HEALTHY MIND/HEALTHY BODY

Before you next do some exercise, spend a few
minutes taking the following test. The answers are on page 73.
Keep a note of your score, and how long you took.

THE BEFORE TEST
1   $26 + 17 = ?$
2   $42 - 9 = ?$
3   $7 \times 4 = ?$
4   What number comes next: 3 10 17 24 ?
5   Which is the odd one out: car, elephant, bicycle, table, cat?
6   Which word goes after news and before aeroplane?
7   Which word is the opposite of warm:
                    hot, shiver, like, cool, south?
8) Which letter comes next: c f i l ?

Now, go and do some exercise for at least half an hour. When
you've finished, as soon as you've got your breath back, take
this second test. The answers are on page 73. How well did
you do this time? Compare your score, and your speed. It's
likely that you did even better, thanks to the extra oxygen
being pumped to your brain.

THE AFTER TEST
1   $16 + 8 = ?$
2   $30 - 7 = ?$
3   $5 \times 9 = ?$
4   Which number comes next: 20 15 10 5 ?
5   Which of these words mean the same:
                    walk, rest, freeze, relax, take?
6) Which word goes before pot, petal, bed and girl?
7) What is the opposite of give: lose, work, take, in, present?
8) Which letter comes next in this sequence: r q p o ?

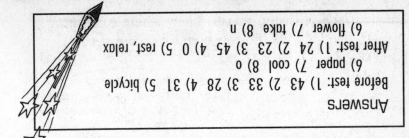

But don't worry if – ....

You're wrong if you think that geniuses are all perfect,
well-rounded individuals, good at everything. Many
had to battle with real problems. Geniuses are just
very good at overcoming obstacles – and with
persistence you can get over just about anything.

Physicist Stephen Hawking is virtually paralysed,
moves around in a wheelchair and speaks only with
the help of a computer. He wrote one of the most
successful books ever, and leads the world to new
levels of understanding. Edison and Beethoven both
lost their hearing, Alexander the Great and Julius
Caesar both suffered epileptic fits – and yet they all
achieved greatness.

Maths genius Paul Erdos was terribly absent-minded
and untidy. Archimedes was said to be so forgetful
that he often missed meals. Inventor Trevor Baylis
works in a particularly untidy room. He recently
described it as 'the sort of place where, if vandals
broke in, they'd leave it looking as though someone
had dropped by to tidy up'!

Einstein had a particularly untidy mind, and a chaotic
workroom. Nobody was allowed to dust or tidy up,
and it looked a complete mess – to everyone except

73

Einstein, who insisted that he knew where everything was. In his daily life, however, he was often very forgetful.

As we've already seen (page 41), Einstein was also bad at maths. In fact, many of the great geniuses failed at particular subjects. Michael Faraday couldn't do even simple sums, and it's not surprising that many great thinkers were dismissed as failures by their teachers. Charles Darwin got very bad reports at school, and still went on to discover amazing things about life on Earth. Trevor Baylis was made to think he was 'a complete dunce at lessons'.

But no matter how many obstacles they have to get around, truly great geniuses will always make it. It's in their character to succeed.

CHAPTER EIGHT

GENIUS THINKING

You have an incredible brain. To be a genius, you need to start using it like a genius.

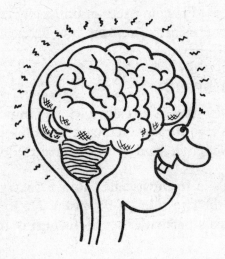

Your brain weighs about 1.4 kg and contains around 12 trillion nerve cells. It can perform millions of operations every second.

Boys have bigger brains than girls, but this doesn't mean that they are any smarter. We all have more than enough brainpower. The most important thing is how well we use it.

After he died in 1955, Albert Einstein's brain was removed and preserved in a laboratory. Scientists were fascinated to see whether it was particularly large or unusually formed in some way.

What scientists discovered was that Einstein's was a perfectly normal brain, but that he had used it in a particular way.

He had formed many more connections between brain cells than other people. His thinking methods were very good for linking things together, learning from everything, and coming up with new solutions and exciting ideas. Einstein used an unusually large proportion of his brain, making him an excellent 'whole brain thinker'.

Your two brains.....................................

Did you know that you really have two brains – a left brain and a right brain? Geniuses like Einstein use both sides together, and you can learn to do that too.

In the 1960s, a scientist called Roger Sperry discovered the two sides of the brain. He found that each side has a particular set of 'favourite' functions.

The left side is where the brain mostly handles:

The right side tends to look after:

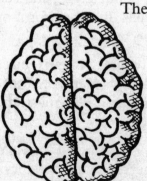

* words
* numbers
* lists
* decisions
* plans

* colours
* ideas
* shapes
* dreaming
* imagination

He discovered that the cleverest and most successful people were good at using both sides of their brain at once.

Small children tend to be more 'right-brained'. They think in pictures and stories, and enjoy playing and experimenting with their imagination.

Adults, on the other hand, are usually much more 'left-brained' and logical. They make lists, count things and make decisions.

Geniuses tend to be somewhere in between. The more of your brain that you can use at any one time, the more powerful your thinking will be.

Some whole-brain thinkers

Leonardo da Vinci was a great painter, but he planned his work very carefully. He made detailed notes about the colours, and worked out the measurements and proportions with great care. His notebooks are full of intricate sketches and notes. ➤

Painting is more right-brain thinking (colours, shapes, spaces, imagination), but planning and preparation is more left-brain (numbers, measurements, decisions, facts). So Leonardo was using both sides of his brain at once, creating amazing pictures like the Mona Lisa.

Of course he was also a great inventor. Again, you can look in his notebooks to find his drawings of tanks, aircraft, diving equipment and so on — but what you notice most is the artistic way in which he sketched them. His work is covered with doodles and scribbles, people, animals, patterns ... Once again he was doing right brain thinking (pictures, ideas, doodles) and left-brain thinking (plans, details, numbers) at the same time. No wonder he came up with so many incredible inventions!

Scientists Isaac Newton and Thomas Edison both used artistic sketches and doodles to help them think. Beethoven's manuscripts include drawings and scribbled ideas amongst the notes. Painter Pablo Picasso made some very detailed mechanical drawings as well as wildly imaginative masterpieces.

Excellent work, Picasso. If you keep this up, you'll make a fine engineer one day.

And Albert Einstein used to use his imagination to help him with his scientific investigations. He once pictured himself riding on a beam of light holding a clock, to help him work out the connection between speed and time. He was an expert in switching on both the logical and the imaginative sides of his brain at once.

Become a whole-brain thinker.................

Use your right brain. Make your written work as imaginative as possible. Use different colours whenever you can. Sketch out your ideas in doodles, patterns and dreamy pictures. At the same time, use your left brain. Keep your work organized, and pay attention to details. Make lists, draw diagrams, and label everything carefully.

To help you solve tricky problems, use your imagination. Picture yourself inside the problem, as if it was a dream. Let your mind wander to amazing new places, and you might be surprised at the answers you come up with. Perhaps singing at the same time helps, or drawing a cartoon to represent your ideas.

Feel free to doodle, make a model or play a musical instrument. Activate your right brain to help with problem solving – don't leave it all to your logical left side.

When you want to come up with ideas for stories, plays, pictures or poems, bring your left brain in to help. Make clear lists of all the ideas you have, then perhaps you could give them all marks out of ten for brilliance. Draw diagrams, make calculations, and do some careful planning. Using your left brain like this gives you extra thinking power.

Become a genius–
BOOST YOUR MEMORY

WHAT YOU'LL NEED

✳ a pen   ✳ some paper

WHAT TO DO

1   Read this shopping list through for one minute:

bananas		jam
milk		bread
sausages		bin liners
chocolate		sprouts
tissues		sweets

Many great geniuses have had incredible memories.
They learnt lots of facts and figures, and kept up to date with
the latest ideas.

The trick is to organize information into lists (left brain), then
use your imagination to turn the lists into stories (right brain).

2   Now cover up the list and write down as many of the
    things on the list as you can remember.
3   Now uncover the list.

What happens? How did you do?

One way to learn the list would be to use your imagination —
and turn it into a strange story:

Imagine peeling a banana, and finding that
inside the skin there was nothing but milk,
which runs down your hands. The milk
pours out across the floor, and you notice
that there are sausages floating in it !

The river of milk reaches a waterfall, and the sausages drop down into a pool of thick, runny chocolate. The chocolate splashes into your face, and you need to wipe it away with a tissue. But the tissues are covered in jam, and you end up in an even stickier mess than before! The only other thing nearby is a slice of bread. Imagine how the bread feels against your face. You toss the bread away into a bin-liner — but it bounces out, because the bin-liner is full of mouldy sprouts. They smell terrible! You lift one out and it transforms into a tasty sweet, and you pop it in your mouth.

Spend a couple of minutes going back through this story. Picture it all happening to you. Imagine the sights, sounds, smells, tastes and textures of this weird tale. Now, can you remember the ten items on the shopping list? The story started with you peeling open a banana!

You can do this trick with anything you need to remember. Simply make a list of words, then write a little story in your mind to link them all together. With practice you can remember hundreds of things!

Some other good memory tips ....

Be observant and alert. You won't remember things unless you've seen or heard them in the first place.

If you can't remember a word or name, run through the alphabet in your mind. Ask yourself whether it begins with a, or b, or c ... and so on, until you jog your memory.

What do you look like when you're straining to remember? Do you have any habits, like scratching your head, rubbing your chin or folding your arms? If you do, then make sure you always do these things when you need to remember something quickly.

Smells are very useful for bringing back memories. If you forget something, try to remember what you could smell when you last saw or heard it. For example, if you were washing your face when you had a good idea, but you've forgotten the idea now, you could sniff a bar of soap to help boost your brain!

Leave yourself reminders. Write on your hand, tie a knot in the corner of your handkerchief, ask other people to remind you ... Always be on the lookout for easy ways to remember everything.

Remember to improve memory

Creative thinking ....

Start using your memory like this, and you'll give
your imagination an excellent workout. Imagination
is vital to genius thinking. Geniuses rely on their
imaginations to have amazing creative thoughts.

Look at this picture.
What do you think it is?

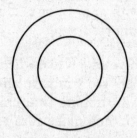

Most people reply to this question with a single
answer, but there are many possible answers.
It could be an eye, a fried egg, a punctured football,
a wheel, a circular door and doorknob, a cowboy hat
from above, a doughnut, a rubber ring – there's no
end to the possibilities.

These are just some of the possibilities. I'm sure you
could come up with more – just as soon as you see
that there's no right (or wrong) answer. All you have
to do is use your imagination.

Never assume anything ....

Always keep an open mind. Scientific geniuses like
Isaac Newton and Stephen Hawking have always
looked for fresh ideas. They were brave enough to
challenge the experts who had gone before, and to see
what they could discover for themselves. Other people
may have found answers, but they're not necessarily
the only answers.

Become a genius— FIND NEW WAYS OF DOING THINGS (1)

WHAT YOU'LL NEED
✱ a book or a magazine

WHAT TO DO
Pick three sentences from your book or magazine. Your challenge is to re-write each sentence so that the new version means exactly the same as the original. The only rule is that you can't use any of the original words! You need to think of new ways to say the same things. It doesn't matter if the new version sounds a bit complicated. It's all excellent practice in seeing new possibilities. For example, if one of the lines reads:

'The two boys left home at 8.45 and boarded the bus for school.'

... you might re-write it as:

'A couple of lads departed their house when clocks read a quarter to nine, then took their coach-seats towards their place of learning.'

An individual little pace for a chap, a single massive bound for everyone.

Reverse things.....................................

Many great ideas have come when people imagined things backwards, or thought about opposites. For example, how do you make a busy road junction safer? One local council thought in reverse, and made the junction even busier by letting the traffic approach from every direction. This slowed down the traffic, made everyone take great care at the junction – and there were fewer accidents!

Become a genius–
FIND NEW WAYS OF DOING THINGS (2)

WHAT TO DO
Come up with as many answers as you can for the following questions:

- How might you smash an egg?
- What could you use to waste water in your home?
- How could you make your school as gloomy as possible?

Now that you've thought in reverse, turn the questions around and answer them again. You'll find that the answers you gave the first time will help you come up with brilliant ideas now:

- Design a device for preventing eggs from getting broken.
- How could you conserve water at home?
- What could you do to make your school a fun place to be?

Take another look ....

Geniuses need to be able to see problems from different angles. Your first attempt to crack a puzzle may not be the best way.

There are often quick ways of solving problems. Try approaching them from different angles.

Boost your senses......................................

Leonardo da Vinci once said that that the average person looks without seeing, listens without hearing, touches without feeling, eats without tasting and inhales without smelling. Leonardo had amazing senses, and used them to explore the world, and to be inspired by it.

The better your senses, the more likely you are to become a genius. Spend time practising the art of seeing, hearing, touching, smelling and tasting.

Become a genius—
BOOST YOUR SENSES

SEEING

1   Spend ten seconds focusing on something in the far distance ... then switch to looking at something close to you. Repeat this change of focus five times. Next, sit by a window and see what you can see. Spend ten minutes picking out as many different colours outside as you can.

2   Rub your hands together for about 15 seconds, then cup your palms over your closed eyes. Relax in this position for two minutes, then take your hands away — but keep your eyes closed. Now slowly open your eyes. The world will seem brighter, the colours sharper. Practise this technique at the start and end of every day to keep your eyesight strong and clear.

HEARING

1   What can you hear at this moment? Spend two minutes noting every different sound you can pick up.

2   Experiment by listening to different sorts of music while you're working. Which music helps your thinking most? On the other hand, perhaps silence is what you prefer?

TOUCHING

1   Practise your touch skills with a friend.
    Close your eyes while your friend places
    different objects in your hand. Can you guess
    what each one is? Swap over so that you can challenge
    your friend, and try to come up with unusual textures.

2   Choose five different textures, and try to describe them in
    as many different ways as possible. Use the most
    descriptive words you can think of.

SMELLING

1   Close your eyes and try to imagine the following smells:
    bacon frying, chocolate, the countryside, smelly cheese, an
    animal.
2   How many different smells can you pick up in the room
    where you're sitting now? It might help to wander around.

TASTING

1   The next time you eat a meal, see how many different
    flavours you can pick out. Can you identify any of the
    individual ingredients?
2   Imagine these tastes as vividly as you can: orange-juice,
    chips, celery, cake, tomato sauce.

CHAPTER NINE

The Genius Challenge

After reading about some of the greatest thinkers, and learning plenty of their secrets, how close are you to becoming a genius? The Genius Challenge will tell you.

You have half an hour to complete the following questions. Before you start, spend a few moments relaxing your mind. Make sure you're feeling alert and positive. Use paper and pens to work with. Prepare to use all the skills you've learnt to think clearly and creatively. Work out what each question is asking you, and think of the best way to respond. You can play music, walk about, juggle, or do anything you like to help your thought process.

You're not helping *my* thought processes!

Use your whole brain, and think like a genius.

Become a genius–
GENIUS CHALLENGE

1 Observation

a) How many edges does a 50-pence piece have?

b) Which of these is the right shape for a Give Way sign at the roadside?

A B C D

c) What's wrong with this picture?

2 Words

a) Which two words in this list mean the same:

loud dull boring hitting sorry?

b) Which word is the odd one out:

loop part shell deer keep?

c) Which word comes after 'rain' and before 'hook'?

3 Numbers

a) Which is the odd one out:

621 245 711 342 ?

b) Which number comes next

1 2 4 7 11 ?

c) If 5389 becomes 8953, then 4067 becomes...? ➤

4 Shapes
Which shape comes next in this sequence?

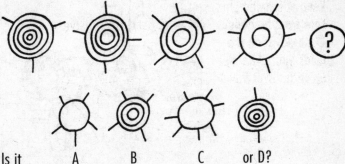

Is it   A   B   C   or D?

5 Memory
Spend a few minutes learning these words, then cover the page and write down as many of them as you can remember:

book, water, watch, baby, CD, hammer, car, elephant, cake, sun

6 Logic
Ben has only two pets. One of his pets is a dog. Charlotte has a cat called Blackie. Blackie loves sardines.

From those details only, which of the following facts is definitely true?
a) Ben doesn't have a cat.   c) Charlotte's cat is black.
b) Charlotte has a dog.   d) Charlotte's cat will eat fish.

7 Creativity
a) What could this be?
   Think of as many different
   answers as you can.

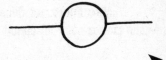

➤

93

b) How could you keep your school free from litter. How many ideas can you come up with?

c) How could you keep your bedroom safe from burglars? Write down all the ideas you come up with.

Now, what was that number again?

8 Puzzles

a) Two Australians are standing on a beach. One is tall and the other is small. The small Australian is the tall Australian's son, but the tall Australian is not the small Australian's father. How can that be possible?

b) Which is heavier: a kilogram of iron or a kilogram of grass?

c) What has a bottom at the top?

Answers

Questions 1–4: award yourself 2 points for each correct answer.

1 a) 7 b) c c) The steam is blowing the wrong way.

2 a) 'dull' and 'boring' b) shell c) coat

3 a) 245 b) 16 c) 6740   4 c

5 Give yourself 1 point for every word you remembered.

6 You get 2 points if your answer is D.

7 Award yourself 1 point for each good idea. Perhaps you could ask a friend to decide which ones might work.

8 3 points for every right answer:

a) The tall Australian is the small Australian's mother.

b) They weigh the same.   c) Your leg!

Genius scores.....................................

How far along the road to genius have you come?

0–20 points: You have a lot of work to do, but you can improve dramatically if you follow the examples set by the geniuses in this book. Read the book again and make sure you try all the experiments and tests. Try to have fun boosting your brainpower, and don't be put off: your journey to genius is only just beginning.

21–40 points:  You've made a good start, but you'll need to master more skills before you can come closer to genius. Set yourself targets to improve, and try to find other books about thinking and brainpower. You've proved you've got what it takes, so make sure you go all the way!

41–60 points: This is a very good score, and shows that you are already thinking like a genius. Make a note of the questions where you lost points, and give those areas a little more attention. Be proud of your amazing brain, and keep up the good work.

61–80 points: Excellent work. With a little more practice, you're going to achieve some incredible things. Spend a little time improving your thinking zone, and perhaps learn to juggle to release your imagination. You've learnt a great deal from this book: now is your chance to start putting it all into practice.

More than 80 points:

Congratulations! You are doing everything right, and there's no reason why you can't become a famous genius. You need to decide where to concentrate your brainpower, but make sure that you explore a variety of interests to keep you inspired. Find other people who think like geniuses, and swap tips and ideas. Keep practising all the techniques explained in this book, and never miss an opportunity for learning. Your score on this test proves that you can be a genius.

THE GENIUS RACES